BETHANY

BETHANY

⊰ A PLAY ⊱

LAURA MARKS

NORTHWESTERN UNIVERSITY PRESS

EVANSTON, ILLINOIS

Northwestern University Press
www.nupress.northwestern.edu

LIBRARY OF CONGRESS
CATALOGING-IN-PUBLICATION DATA

Marks, Laura, 1972– author.
    Bethany : a play / Laura Marks.
        pages cm
        ISBN 978-0-8101-2998-6 (pbk. : alk.
paper)
    I. Title.
PS3613.A7646B48 2014
812.6—dc23
                                2013050524

∞ The paper used in this publication meets
the minimum requirements of the American National Standard for Information Sci-
ences—Permanence of Paper for Printed
Library Materials, ANSI Z39.48-1992.

Printed in the United States of America

10 9 8 7 6 5 4 3 2 1

For Eleanor and Clarissa, always.

Do you know the definition of charisma?
Believing in your own bullshit!
—Lukas Foss

CONTENTS

ACKNOWLEDGMENTS

Mike Levine and Anne Gendler at Northwestern University Press, and freelance editor Elizabeth Levenson.

Julie Crosby and everyone at the Women's Project.

The phenomenal cast, crew, and creative team of the original production, especially the brilliant Gaye Taylor Upchurch.

Jessica Amato and everyone at Gersh.

Beloved teachers Marsha Norman and Christopher Durang. Also at Juilliard: Tanya Barfield and my kick-ass classmates.

Everyone at the Public Theater, especially Liz Frankel.

The Leah Ryan Fund for Emerging Women Writers, the Fellowship of Southern Writers, the Helen Merrill Fund, the Susan Smith Blackburn Prize, and New Dramatists.

The many, many people and companies who supported the development life of this play: the Lark, Steppenwolf, MTC, Reverie, Synchronicity, APAC, Partial Comfort, the Wilma, the Barrow Street, HighTide, Naked Angels, and a wealth of talented actors and directors.

Davis McCallum. It's his fault I started writing plays.

My parents, for their love and encouragement.

Most of all, Ken Marks. What a joy it was to do this with you.

PRODUCTION HISTORY

The world premiere of *Bethany* was in January 2013, presented by Women's Project Theater (under the direction of Julie Crosby and Lisa Fane) at New York City Center Stage II. It was directed by Gaye Taylor Upchurch, with scenic design by Lauren Helpern, costume design by Sarah J. Holden, lighting design by Mark Barton, and sound design by Leon Rothenberg. Fight direction was by J. David Brimmer. The production stage manager was Jess Johnston. The play, by Laura Marks, was developed at the Lark Play Development Center, New York City.

Charlie . . . . Ken Marks

Crystal . . . . America Ferrera

Gary . . . . Tobias Segal

Shannon . . . . Emily Ackerman

Toni . . . . Myra Lucretia Taylor

Patricia . . . . Kristin Griffith

BETHANY

CHARACTERS

Charlie
Crystal
Gary
Shannon
Toni
Patricia

TIME

Early 2009

PLACE

The exurbs of a small city in America

PROLOGUE

[A middle-aged man stands facing out, giving a speech. His style is presentational, yet intimate and folksy—think Rick Warren at Saddleback.]

CHARLIE: There's a reason you're here today. You might not believe that, but I do. You see, there's a higher power that guides our destiny. I don't care if you call it God or Yahweh or Uncle Fred, doesn't matter. And I'll tell you one thing about this higher power: He wants you to be rich. Rich beyond your wildest dreams. He doesn't want you to lie awake all night, wondering how you're gonna make that mortgage payment when your kid's college tuition is due and your credit cards are already maxed to the limit. You know, last year, in the town where I live, over thirty-five thousand people lost their homes to foreclosure. Thirty-five thousand! There are some neighborhoods where you can go for a walk and you won't hardly see *anyone.* And do you know what's the saddest part about all that? Those people could have saved their homes . . . if they'd known the secrets that I'm about to share with you today. These secrets are as old as the hills, and more powerful than a thunderstorm. They're the reason that I live in a beautiful five-bedroom home with a hot tub, and a flat-screen TV, and everything else a man could ever want. If you've been living a life based on hard work, and anxiety, or even fear, your life is about to change forever. So if you haven't already, open up your notebooks; and while you're at it, open up your minds.

[*He pauses for a moment and peers straight ahead—straightens his tie, picks food out of his teeth. It's clear now that he's actually been giving this speech to himself, in a mirror.*]

CHARLIE: That's when I should do that thing with the kazoos.

SCENE ONE

[*Night. The empty, eat-in kitchen of a small house in the suburbs. Built-in cabinets but no furniture. The counters are bare except for a pile of mail. After some lengthy fumbling with the sliding glass door, a woman enters from outside. She has a small wheeled suitcase, purse, and garment bag. She's conservatively dressed, in a suit jacket, skirt, and heels, and attractive.*

She puts down her things. She's cautious, listening. Turns on the small light over the stove. Quickly looks through the pile of mail. She opens the refrigerator and realizes it's not running. As she kneels down to check the plug, she suddenly stops.]

CRYSTAL: Hello?

[*No answer. She plugs in the fridge. There's an audible hum as it starts to run. She opens the refrigerator again, and this time the light comes on. It takes a few seconds for her to notice the man who has silently entered the room.*]

CRYSTAL:	GARY:
Oh my God—	It's okay—
Oh, I'm so sorry—	Shh. It's okay, I'm going—

CRYSTAL: You know? I think—I, I, I must have just wandered into the wrong house by mistake, I'm so terribly sorry, I'll just be on my—

[*A long moment while they stare at each other.*]

[*Grabbing something from her purse*]: I have pepper spray.

GARY: I won't hurt you.

CRYSTAL: I'll just get my things here—

GARY: You don't have to go. I'm leaving right now.

CRYSTAL: What are you saying?

GARY: It's okay. You don't have to call the police.

CRYSTAL: I'm sorry, what's the deal? Do you live here?

GARY: No. Do you?

CRYSTAL : . . . Yes. I mean—not exactly, but my friend. It belongs to my friend.

GARY: What's his name?

CRYSTAL: Joe. Parker.

[*Pause.* GARY *laughs.*]

What?

GARY: You got that from looking at the mail.

CRYSTAL: It's true. Joe is my boyfriend.

GARY: Joe is eighty.

[*Pause.*]

CRYSTAL: What are you doing here?

GARY: I just need a place to lay my head. I won't bother you. You won't need your "pepper spray."

[*Pause.*]

CRYSTAL: It's really just breath spray.

[*She sprays some in her mouth.*]

Fresh breath is important in my line of work.

GARY: What do you do?

CRYSTAL: Sales. You?

[*He laughs. From the looks of him, he hasn't held a job in quite a while. She laughs too, nervously.*]

GARY: What?

[*She shuts the refrigerator door.*]

CRYSTAL: It's good that the electric still works. He's only been gone a few days, right?

GARY: More like a week.

CRYSTAL: That makes sense. Who wants to wait around for the marshals?

GARY: Do you know how much he owed?

CRYSTAL: No.

GARY: Two hundred and fifty-four thousand.

CRYSTAL: Unbelievable. Did he have a line of credit?

GARY: How can people be so dumb?

CRYSTAL: He might have been sick.

GARY: He might have been stupid.

CRYSTAL: Well, why don't you go buy a house someday and show us all how it works.

[*Pause. She backs away slightly.*]

GARY: Do I smell bad?

CRYSTAL: No—not really, I can't really tell—

GARY: I haven't been showering.

CRYSTAL: Is the water shut off already?

GARY: No. Sometimes I just forget.

[*A pause while she looks at him, weighing her options.*]

CRYSTAL: Where are you sleeping?

GARY: Upstairs. So I guess you could have the downstairs if you want. The living room carpet is pretty soft.

CRYSTAL: How long do you think—I mean—

GARY: Water should stay on until the end of the month. Electric, who knows. Eventually the bank'll put it up for auction, but at this point it might not be worth the trouble.

[*She's silent, considering.*]

CRYSTAL: What's your name?

GARY: Gary.

CRYSTAL: Hi Gary. I'm Crystal.

[*She initiates a handshake. Pause. She reaches into her purse, gets out a packet of nuts, and opens it.*]

Are you hungry? Come here.

[*She hands him the packet. He pours some into his hand and wolfs them down.*]

GARY: Thanks.

[*He offers the packet back to her.*]

CRYSTAL: Go ahead, have the rest. I already had Quiznos.

[*Pause.*]

Oh Christ. I can't do this. Fuck, fuck fuck fuck fuck.

[*She starts frantically gathering her things. A contradictory impulse stops her. She leans on the counter, trying to think.*]

GARY: You don't have to go. I'm pretty harmless. But if you have another option, by all means . . . There's always the park, but people can come and fuck with you in the park. I mean, literally. If I were you, I'd go with the devil you know, so to speak.

[*Pause.*]

Think it over. I'm going upstairs.

CRYSTAL: Are you going to sleep?

GARY: No, probably just a little meditation. Maybe jerk off if I need to. But I don't think I do.

[*Pause.*]

If I do, I'll shut the door.

CRYSTAL: Okay.

GARY: Good night.

[*He leaves. After a moment she slides her purse off her shoulder and sets it down. She digs in the purse and gets out a photograph: it's wallet-sized, like a school picture. She looks at it as the lights dim.*]

SCENE TWO

[*The next day.* CRYSTAL *stands on the sales floor of a Saturn dealership. Light background music.* CHARLIE *stands next to her, holding a couple of glossy spec sheets.*]

CRYSTAL: . . . The two-door XE has a hundred and thirty-eight horse-power engine, five-speed manual transmission, cruise control; it's virtually the same as the XR except that it doesn't have the sixteen-inch alloy wheels or the advanced audio system, or the sport bucket seats with driver-side lumbar, which I'm thinking you might actually need since you say you do a lot of driving. If you want to save fifteen hundred dollars, hey, in this economic climate, I completely understand. But I see that iPod in your pocket so I know you're a man who likes his music, and I gotta say, having all those audio controls right on the steering wheel is an amazing feeling: it's like, you're heading down the highway and you've got the whole world right there . . .

CHARLIE: How did you learn so much about cars? Did your boyfriend teach you?

CRYSTAL: I don't have a boyfriend.

CHARLIE: You really know your stuff. [*Pause.*] I was here about a month ago, but I didn't see you then. Are you new?

[*Her smile abruptly vanishes.*]

CRYSTAL: Did you work with a salesperson the last time you were here?

CHARLIE: A girl named Tammy.

CRYSTAL: Oh no. I should . . . I should probably get Tammy for you then.

CHARLIE: You trying to get rid of me?

CRYSTAL: Oh, God no! I would love to work with you—it's just that we're really not allowed to take each other's customers. It's really complicated, but basically, you see, we work on straight commission—

CHARLIE: How about we just pretend I never told you?

[*She looks around.*]

I don't want to work with her anyway. I'd rather work with you.

[*Pause.*]

Come on. "The customer is always right."

CRYSTAL: I know, but—

CHARLIE: Shhh, I love this song—

[*A new song surges forward on the dealership soundtrack: "Sea of Love," or something equally lush and romantic. They listen to it together for a while.*]

I swear I've seen you somewhere before.

CRYSTAL: I used to work at the Ford dealership.

CHARLIE: No, that's not it.

CRYSTAL: Well, I just have one of those faces; people always think they went to high school with me.

CHARLIE: You were in diapers when I was in high school.

[*Pause.*]

Anyway, I filled out the form.

[*He hands her a thin Lucite clipboard.*]

And here's my card.

[*She looks at it.*]

CRYSTAL: . . . "Transformative Motivational Speaker"—wait a minute. I know you! I went to that free talk you gave at the Holiday Inn.

CHARLIE: See, there you go.

CRYSTAL: I still have my notebook. And I remember when I got home, I made a list of all my bills and put it out to the universe, just like you said.

CHARLIE: And look at you now. You're doing great.

CRYSTAL: Well . . . You know, that same week, I did have a couple of parking tickets and when I went to pay them, they couldn't find one in the computer, so it was free.

CHARLIE: We call that "synchronicity." The more you use the tools, the more it starts to happen.

CRYSTAL: I don't know. I probably wasn't doing it right.

CHARLIE: That lecture was just the tip of the iceberg. You should have signed up for my boot camp. That's where we really get into challenging your assumptions.

CRYSTAL: You know, I just didn't have the money—

CHARLIE: People always say that. It's an investment. But it ends up paying for itself, a hundred times over.

[*Pause.*]

Well, speaking of investments . . . Aren't you gonna offer me a test drive?

CRYSTAL: Would you like to go for a test drive?

[*He gestures for her to go first, and they start off.*]

SCENE THREE

[*Evening of the same day.* CRYSTAL *comes into the kitchen, again through the sliding glass door. This time it's apparent that she's using a thin, plastic ID card to jimmy the lock. She does it more easily now. She has her luggage as before, along with a couple of stuffed, no-label shopping bags and a greasy bag of takeout.*]

CRYSTAL: Gary? Are you still here?

[*He pops up from behind the counter. He's holding a two-by-four.*]

—Oh Jesus—

GARY: Sorry.

CRYSTAL: What the hell is that for?

GARY: Just . . . protection.

CRYSTAL: Protection from what?

[*He thinks for a moment. He gently lays the two-by-four on the counter.*]

I brought hamburgers. Are you hungry?

[*She starts unpacking the bag.*]

GARY: I was just going to fix some C-rations.

CRYSTAL: What are those?

[*He shows her a small cardboard box.*]

GARY: From the Army-Navy store. They keep forever.

CRYSTAL: Well, great, keep it for another night. I'm buying.

GARY: Do you always wear a suit?

CRYSTAL: It's . . . you know. I have to. But I can't afford to get anything dry-cleaned. Pretty soon I'm gonna smell like a . . .

[*Embarrassed silence.*]

GARY: I took a shower.

CRYSTAL: That's great!

[*They start eating picnic-style on the floor.*]

So tell me about your day. Did you go anywhere?

[GARY *shakes his head.*]

It was really nice out.

GARY: I didn't have anywhere to go.

CRYSTAL: Well, I hear you, but you could go hang out at the library, or . . . I don't know . . .

GARY: I mean I didn't *need* to go anywhere.

CRYSTAL: So you don't go anywhere unless you need to?

GARY: Pretty much.

CRYSTAL: Do you have . . . like, a phobia, or something?

[*No answer.*]

I'm sorry, I'm usually not this rude . . .

[*Pause.*]

GARY: I don't like crowds. Crowding is unnatural; it causes stress and aggression. They've proved it with animals.

CRYSTAL: Okay.

[*Pause.*]

Anyway, I had a good day at work. I think, maybe, I've finally met someone who wants to buy a goddamned car.

GARY: Hooray for fossil fuels.

CRYSTAL: Hooray for seven percent commission.

GARY: Is it new, or used?

CRYSTAL: Do I look like the used car type? This guy is strictly top-of-the-line. He's looking at a Sky Red Line, fully loaded.

GARY: I only know cars from the seventies and eighties. Nowadays they make them out of plastic.

CRYSTAL: It's polymer.

GARY: That's because the government is saving the metal. They're hoarding it.

CRYSTAL: What for?

GARY: Think about it. Metal is going to be one of the key substances in the new barter economy. As long as your fire is hot enough, you can make metal do whatever you want. Plastic just melts and turns into poison.

CRYSTAL: Okay.

GARY: You should take your seven percent commission and invest in a scrap-metal yard.

[*She laughs.*]

CRYSTAL: You know . . . investing is not really my top priority right now.

[*She starts unpacking the shopping bags, stocking the kitchen with various things: paper towels, china plates, and cutlery from Goodwill.*]

GARY: Don't tell me you're gonna go rent some apartment. That's just throwing money away.

CRYSTAL: So how does it work: you just stay someplace until the water gets turned off, and then you go and try to find some other house?

GARY: There's always another house; the hard part is finding one with lights and water. Take a look outside. You see any lights in those houses? It's a ghost town.

[*She looks out the glass door for a long while, realizing how alone they are.*]

CRYSTAL: That streetlight's not on.

[*Pause.*]

> Well, at least it's quiet. You can see the stars. Did you ever do any camping? I mean . . . voluntarily? I went once. I couldn't believe the sky. Like it was just dusted with white.

GARY: Plenty more where that came from. The days of trying to get "back to nature"—that's all over. Nature's coming back to us.

CRYSTAL: What do you mean?

GARY: These cheap-ass houses—they're just scrap now. We're sitting in a drywall junkyard. Pretty soon you're gonna see squirrels nesting in these cabinets. Vines crawling over the floor.

CRYSTAL: That's insane.

GARY: You'll see people start to change too. Fighting to survive. It doesn't bring out the best in a person.

[*Pause.*]

CRYSTAL: Listen: I need to ask a couple of favors of you.

GARY: This oughta be good.

CRYSTAL: Will you be home during the day tomorrow?

[*He nods.*]

> Okay, good. I'm having some stuff delivered. Just a table and chair set, from Goodwill. I just need someone here to open the door. And the other thing is even easier. The day after tomorrow, I have this appointment. This person needs to come over and see where I live. So I was wondering if you could maybe just . . . not be here.

GARY: That's a problem.

CRYSTAL: Just for a couple of hours. You could go for a walk, or run some errands . . . It's not like you'd run into crowds or anything.

GARY: What time?

CRYSTAL: Afternoon.

GARY: No way.

CRYSTAL: Come on. You must go out all the time to get your C-rations or whatever.

GARY: Only when I *need* to.

CRYSTAL: Please, Gary, I can't—I can't even begin to tell you how important this is.

GARY: Do you seriously expect me to go out and wander around the neighborhood for *two hours*?

CRYSTAL: So go to the library.

GARY: You and that fucking library! No. No way. I see your MO. You buy me a hamburger like I'm your buddy, and now you want to kick me out and change the locks on me. I was here first, lady.

CRYSTAL: I'm really hurt that you would think that, Gary. I've never been anything but nice to you. And you've been so kind to me, letting me stay here. I don't know if I could do this if I didn't have you here to help me. I appreciate it so much.

[*Pause.*]

GARY: What if I just stay upstairs?

CRYSTAL: They need to see the whole house.

GARY: Who does?

CRYSTAL: It's complicated.

GARY: Why can't you just say, "This is my friend, Gary"? I'll take a shower.

CRYSTAL: Because they'll assume that I'm involved with you.

GARY: And that would be deeply embarrassing to you; I get it. Because I'm such a disgusting specimen—

CRYSTAL: No, I swear, you could be Brad Pitt—I mean, you're perfectly attractive, as far as I can tell, but I absolutely cannot look like I'm involved with anyone or living with anyone. At all.

[Pause.]

GARY: Okay. So, I got it. I'll be the plumber.

CRYSTAL: What?

GARY: Like they say in the porno films: "I'm just here to fix the sink."

CRYSTAL: . . . Do you . . . do you have any tools, or anything?

GARY: One or two. I can improvise.

CRYSTAL: I don't know.

GARY: It's a good cover. And you know, if you're having the place worked on, it helps it look like you really live here. Because a table and chair set isn't gonna cut it.

CRYSTAL: I bought other things too, like toilet paper and some sheets to put on the bed, I mean, *your* bed. I'll say that I just moved in.

GARY: That's true enough.

CRYSTAL: Gary, don't take this the wrong way, but I need to know that you're not gonna screw this up. If we do this, you have to be completely quiet. Let me do all the talking.

GARY: I know what I'm doing. I've been living under the radar for a long time.

CRYSTAL: Okay! We're a team, right?

[GARY *starts sliding his pants down.*]

What the hell are you doing?

GARY: Just . . . that's how the plumbers wear their jeans . . . 'Cause when they bend over—

CRYSTAL: Okay, that's too far.

GARY: Just trying to look realistic . . .

CRYSTAL: You should go to bed now.

GARY: You're not the boss of me.

CRYSTAL: I didn't mean—oh God, that's such a mom thing. I'm—I'm sorry.

[CRYSTAL *quickly turns away and busies herself in the kitchen.* GARY *watches her, then gathers up his remaining food and his two-by-four.*]

GARY: Hey. It's all fine. I'm not gonna screw anything up. I don't want you to worry.

[*She tries to smile.*]

CRYSTAL: Good night.

GARY: Good night.

[*He exits.*]

SCENE FOUR

[CHARLIE *stands alone, practicing a speech in his mirror.*]

CHARLIE: What do you want?

[*He points to an imaginary person as if calling on someone and holds for their response, which he repeats.*]

"More money." Okay. Come here a minute.

[*To himself*] I have to make sure I have a nickel.

Here's a nickel. Now you're richer than when you came in. Seriously, though—anyone have a more specific answer?

[CHARLIE *calls on people, as before.*]

"More sales." "More commissions." Ah. "I want to be rich." Okay, let's hold for a minute. This is my favorite answer: "I Want To Be Rich." Let me ask you this: Why do you want to be rich? Why? "So you don't have to worry anymore." More answers, come on: "So you won't lose your house." "Medical expenses." "So your wife will respect you." "So you can buy things." Okay, stop. Let me ask you this. What things? Uh-uh, don't tell me. Close your eyes. Now visualize the first thing that comes to mind. How big is it? What color is it? Is the light hitting it in a special way? Now stretch out your hand—can you see your hand?—and run your fingers over it. How does it feel? Now come right up next to it, and see if you can press your face against it, what does it smell like? What does *she* smell like? Ha, just kidding. Now: I want you to say something to yourself. Don't say, "I want this." Say: "This Is Mine."

SCENE FIVE

[*Sounds of rain and thunder. Lights rise on* SHANNON, *a woman in her thirties, who stands on the sales floor of the dealership reviewing a checklist on a clipboard.* CRYSTAL *rushes in. She's soaked.*]

CRYSTAL: Sorry I'm late, I took the—

SHANNON: Did you punch in?

CRYSTAL: No, I'll go do it right now.

SHANNON: Do it later. You have a customer.

CRYSTAL: No way.

SHANNON: He's in the men's room. Are you . . . ?

CRYSTAL: What?

SHANNON: Is something up?

CRYSTAL: I'm fine. Do I look all right?

SHANNON: We need to talk when you have a second.

CRYSTAL: Sure.

[SHANNON *moves away as* CHARLIE *walks in with a newspaper.*]

CHARLIE: . . . There's my girl.

CRYSTAL: Wow, you're a real early bird.

CHARLIE: Do I need to buy you an umbrella?

CRYSTAL: It's weird, I can never manage to keep one.

[*He takes off his raincoat and puts it around her shoulders.*]

CHARLIE: Here you go.

CRYSTAL: Thank you.

CHARLIE: I was getting cold just looking at you.

[*Pause.*]

CRYSTAL: So . . . are we doing your contract today?

CHARLIE: I was thinking I'd like to see how that car handles in the rain.

CRYSTAL: You're a smart shopper. I like that.

CHARLIE: Well, it's a big investment.

CRYSTAL: Absolutely. A car is like your second skin. Well, I'll get you the keys and you can go spend the whole day out there if you want.

CHARLIE: You free to ride shotgun?

CRYSTAL: Oh gee, I'd love to, but I, uh, I have this meeting with my supervisor.

CHARLIE: I don't mind waiting. You all have free coffee in the lounge.

CRYSTAL: . . . Okay then. Great. I'll come find you.

[He exits.]

SHANNON: What's his deal?

CRYSTAL: He's pre-qualified.

SHANNON: A twelve-year-old can get pre-qualified.

CRYSTAL: What did you want to talk about?

SHANNON: We're closing.

CRYSTAL: Closing early?

SHANNON: No, closing forever. The service center's hanging on for a little while, but the sales floor is toast.

CRYSTAL: Oh my God.

SHANNON: So if you're working on any deals you need to close 'em by the end of the week.

CRYSTAL: Why didn't you tell me before?

SHANNON: Crystal, get a grip, okay? We've been operating in the red for two straight quarters, half the associates are gone; what did you think was gonna happen?

CRYSTAL: But that's not what you do in a change cycle; you have to— you have to hang in there, you know? Because times like these are all about thinning the herd, and that's good for us, but we have to ride it out, we have to; it's all just—it's just part of the cycle.

SHANNON: You sound like my 401(k) guy.

CRYSTAL: Did you talk to headquarters? Because all they have to do is find someone else to buy out the franchise, this is crazy—

SHANNON: HQ doesn't give two shits about it. They're busy trying to sell the whole company.

CRYSTAL: What? Who could they sell it to?

SHANNON: I don't know. Japanese.

[*Pause.*]

CRYSTAL: Shannon, I just want to say . . . If we get any more walk-ins . . . I know today, with the rain—but tomorrow morning, I'm here, or Thursday or Friday . . . Shannon, please, I was salesperson of the month twice in a row when I was at Ford. If anyone else walks through that door, you give that person to me and I will close them. You know I will. I will absolutely close them, and I will give you, personally, twenty-five percent of my commission.

[*Pause.*]

SHANNON: Did you steal a customer from Tammy?

CRYSTAL: No, I—

SHANNON: Because she told me you did.

CRYSTAL: It's not . . . no, it wasn't like that, this guy just—

SHANNON: Whatever, I don't wanna hear excuses, but you know what? Tammy's husband is on disability. And she may not be as pretty as you, but she's been here a heck of a lot longer and worked her butt off. So if we get any walk-ins, which at this point is about as likely as Pluto crash-landing into the parking lot, I think I'm gonna give them to Tammy. Because you know what? There's a special place in hell for women who don't help other women.

[SHANNON *exits. After a moment,* CRYSTAL *slips the borrowed coat off her shoulders and looks at it. It's an expensive raincoat. She reads the designer label in the collar, folds the coat over her arm, and exits to go find* CHARLIE.]

SCENE SIX

[*The next day. The kitchen. The table and chair set has arrived.* GARY *kneels in front of the open sink cabinet, wrench in hand. He starts futzing convincingly with the pipes when he hears* CRYSTAL *coming down from upstairs along with* TONI, *an alert, fortyish woman in a muted pants set.*]

TONI [*making notes in a folder*]: So the living room, we saw.

CRYSTAL: I wanted to get a couch, but they said it takes eight weeks.

TONI: Not a problem. I'd rather see you wait eight weeks than go to one of those rental places. I had a client get bedbugs.

CRYSTAL: Oh my God.

TONI: You mind if I look in your fridge?

[CRYSTAL *nods, and she does.*]

All right, I'd like to see more fresh vegetables in here, but I know you just moved in. Cleaning products?

CRYSTAL: Oh sure, I have . . . let's see . . . Joy, and 409 . . .

TONI: Where do you store your cleaning products?

CRYSTAL: I . . .

TONI: Under the sink?

CRYSTAL: No.

TONI: Never under the sink. Not even if you have one of those little door latches.

CRYSTAL: Absolutely—

TONI: Because kids are smart, they figure out how to open those things up in about two minutes.

CRYSTAL: I keep everything up high.

[TONI *goes to the sliding glass door and looks closely at the handle. She sits down at the table.*]

TONI [*writing*]: Let me just catch up on my notes.

CRYSTAL: Take your time.

[CRYSTAL *sits and waits.*]

TONI: Okay. Here's what I still need to see:

[CRYSTAL*'s face falls.*]

Don't get upset on me. You're getting there. You have a pen?

CRYSTAL [*not moving*]: Sure.

[TONI *hands her a pen and paper.*]

TONI: Number one: window guards. On every second floor window. Write that down. You get them at the hardware store, about twenty bucks a pop. Your handyman here probably knows how to put them in. Number two: another bed.

CRYSTAL: I thought she could just share with me for a while.

TONI: You know, she could, but we discourage it. You just don't want to know the stories I've heard. Mostly having to do with the fathers, but still.

CRYSTAL: So, I'm sorry, I don't get it. She's not supposed to be old enough to know not to drink Drano or climb out a second floor window, but she's too old to sleep in her mommy's bed?

TONI: I don't write the standards, I'm just trying to tell you, I know what my supervisor is going to say—

CRYSTAL: All right—

TONI: If you were in a motel that would be one thing, but you have plenty of room so I don't see what the problem—

CRYSTAL: Fine, I'll get a bed.

TONI: Let's say you have a gentleman who wants to spend the night—

CRYSTAL: That's not going to happen. Let's move on.

TONI: That's about it. I'll just need a copy of your lease, for the file.

CRYSTAL: . . . Great.

TONI: Or if you just have the original, I can take it with me and run it off at the office.

CRYSTAL: You know, the landlord still has my copy, so I can just make a copy at work and fax it to you, would that work?

TONI: Everything all right at the Saturn dealership?

CRYSTAL: Yep, it's a great team over there.

[TONI *looks over at* GARY, *who by now has run out of things to do to the pipes. He's just sitting there.*]

TONI: I'd like to ask you about something a little more sensitive.

CRYSTAL: Gary, while you're here, could you also take a look at the upstairs bathroom? The faucet is a little drippy.

GARY: Sure.

[*He exits.*]

TONI: I should get his number from you. Is he reasonable?

CRYSTAL: You know, the landlord is paying so I'm not really sure.

TONI: Crystal, I just need to ask you: do you have any other issues that we should know about? Any addiction problems?

CRYSTAL: No.

TONI: Drugs? Gambling? QVC?

CRYSTAL: No.

TONI: Mental health issues?

CRYSTAL: I went over all this with the other guy—

TONI: I don't care if you did. I'm asking you now.

CRYSTAL: There's nothing wrong with me.

TONI: But you see, when I go back to my supervisor and say, "She's a nice-looking, clean woman who finished school and has a job," he's going to say, "So what exactly is her problem?"

CRYSTAL: My only problem is I lost my house. And when I went to the shelter, you people said, "Sorry, the shelter's full, but why don't we take that little girl off your hands?"

TONI: You can't have a small child sleeping in a car.

CRYSTAL: We only did that for a few nights.

TONI: It's not safe. And it's not right.

[*Pause.*]

I understand you stopped by the school yesterday.

CRYSTAL: I had something I wanted to give her—

[*She goes to get a letter from her purse.*]

TONI: If you don't have custody, you can't just show up at school.

CRYSTAL: I know, I just thought—I mean, they *know* me at her school—

TONI: I thought we were very clear on that.

CRYSTAL: I'm sorry, but—the thing is, I went to the park on Sunday, just like you said, and the family never showed up with her—I ended up sitting there for three hours—

TONI: I know. I've talked to the family. It won't happen again.

CRYSTAL: Can you at least give her this letter? And make sure those people read it to her?

TONI [*taking the letter*]: I'll see what I can do.

CRYSTAL: Is she okay, or does she seem like . . .

TONI: She acts out a little at school, but at home they say she's fine.

CRYSTAL: Oh shit, I forgot the stickers.

[*She gets a sheet of Hello Kitty stickers out of her purse, takes the letter back, and starts feverishly decorating the envelope.*]

TONI: Just bear in mind that we're going to need to open that letter.

CRYSTAL: Why?

TONI: It's just policy, like everything else. And just one piece of advice: I know you'd never say anything intentionally to hurt her, believe me; but we try to discourage parents from making promises they can't keep.

[CRYSTAL *clutches the letter for a moment, but she gives it back to* TONI.]

CRYSTAL: I'm just telling her I've found us a house. And I'm coming to get her soon.

TONI: All right. I'll stop by again on Monday, same time. If everything looks good, then I'll make a recommendation to my supervisor.

CRYSTAL: Great. That's great. Thank you.

[TONI *gets up.*]

I'll walk you out.

TONI: Don't bother, my car is out this way.

[*She heads for the sliding glass door.*]

But when you get a chance . . . you need to get a better lock over here. Anybody can bust this thing open with a credit card.

[TONI *exits. We hear her car starting as* GARY *comes downstairs.*]

GARY: You're in some deep shit.

CRYSTAL: No I'm not—what are you talking about? All I have to do is forge a lease; that's the easiest thing in the world.

[*Pause.*]

You were perfect. Thank you.

GARY: I told you you didn't have to worry about me. See, I'm the kind of guy you want in your foxhole . . . Um, that's a war reference.

[*Pause.*]

You have a kid.

CRYSTAL: I do.

GARY: Interesting.

CRYSTAL: Why?

GARY: I don't know. I guess I didn't think you'd ever done anything worthwhile with your life.

CRYSTAL: Are you serious?

GARY: How old is she?

CRYSTAL: Five. She's in kindergarten.

GARY: Is she moving in?

CRYSTAL: I don't know.

GARY: For a long time I thought having kids was a bad idea, because of overpopulation; but now I think the people who know what's going on should have as many kids as they can, because the revolution won't be over in one person's lifetime.

CRYSTAL: What revolution?

GARY: But you have to choose the right genes. You're a good specimen; I can see why someone wanted to mate with you. You have to be a pretty tough animal to keep your genetic material alive. There's so much that can happen, like you were saying, drinking Drano or—

CRYSTAL: That lady is unbelievable. My kid is five; she knows not to drink the goddamned Drano. And where the hell am I supposed to find two hundred bucks for window guards? And a bed?

[*Pause.*]

Where did you find that bed you have?

GARY: You don't want to know.

CRYSTAL: I just have to make this sale. I have to.

[*She gets out the wallet-sized photograph from before and looks at it.* GARY *comes and looks over her shoulder.*]

GARY: What's her name?

CRYSTAL: Bethany.

[*He takes the picture for a closer look.*]

GARY: What are they teaching her in school?

CRYSTAL: . . . Um, the usual stuff. Two plus two.

GARY: That's what you think.

CRYSTAL: What are you talking about?

GARY: They're socializing her. They're teaching her not to hit other kids, and to keep her skirt down, and to raise her hand when she has to go to the bathroom. Every single thing her body wants to do is getting smashed down by the military-industrial complex, and the worst part is that it happens all day, every day, to everyone, and everyone just lets it happen. Look at you: you go around all day with that big, fake smile pasted across your face, selling people a bunch of crap they don't need so you can go buy crap you don't need. "I just have to make this sale." You completely bought the government messages. But what happens now? Are you gonna just curl up and die? Or are you gonna fight back? Because when you have to struggle for food and shelter, just like we did millions of years ago, boom! You start getting your mind back. And we have to take advantage of this time and fight the system until we obliterate it. You and me, we'll never recover a hundred percent; but your daughter's young; she might still have a chance . . . You see, it won't be a collective society anymore where technology controls the masses. It'll just be individuals and small groups. And when the centers of technology and finance go down, we need to be ready to survive. Small, nomadic groups have the best shot at it. I know how to trap food and I know all the edible plants.

CRYSTAL: That's great.

GARY: You said, "I don't know." How come?

CRYSTAL: I didn't say that.

GARY: No, before when I said, "Is your daughter moving in," you said, "I don't know." How come?

CRYSTAL: I—I haven't decided what to do yet.

GARY: I'll tell you what you should do. You pick her up from school. You say, "Don't worry, honey, we're never going back there again." Then the three of us get in your car and we start driving. We drive until we hit wilderness. Someplace without all this EMF radiation. We build a shelter. Or find one. And we've got the seeds of a new society. XX . . . XX . . . XY.

CRYSTAL: That's really sweet, Gary.

GARY: I'm not being sweet.

CRYSTAL: I have to think about it.

GARY: Yeah, see, that's not a good answer because your mind is full of all that system bullshit. But I'm thinking about your daughter; and if you were thinking about what's best for her long-term survival, you'd be down on your knees thanking me right now.

CRYSTAL: I'm very grateful, I promise, I just—could I have that picture back?

GARY: God, women always act like there's something wrong with me. But every time I go into a public bathroom, some guy tries to blow me. Why is that?

CRYSTAL: Gary, right now we need to focus on getting her back.

GARY: Right.

CRYSTAL: I need your help. I really need it. You were so great today. We just have to stay here for five more days.

[GARY *stiffens and stares out the window at the streetlight, which has started to sputter on uncertainly.*]

What is it? Is someone out there?

GARY: It's happening.

CRYSTAL: What is?

GARY: They know.

CRYSTAL: Who does?

GARY: The government.

CRYSTAL: . . . It's just the streetlight. I think it's broken.

GARY: Don't say that! I know what I'm talking about! Do you want to end up dead?

CRYSTAL: I'm sorry.

[*He turns off the light over the stove.*]

GARY: No lights tonight.

CRYSTAL: I won't. I promise.

GARY: I'll go upstairs and keep a lookout. Think about what I said.

[*He grabs her hand and holds it between his hands for a minute like it's a precious object, then lets go and runs upstairs. Lights fade.*]

SCENE SEVEN

[CHARLIE *is alone at his mirror again. He's carefully tying his tie.*]

CHARLIE: Are you busy after work? Because . . .

[*He revises his approach.*]

> Do you like Mexican? Because . . . You look like you could use a
> good meal. I'll drive. No, don't bother. Save your gas . . . This car's
> been good to me, but it's time to trade up, you know? . . . No, I
> didn't even bring my checkbook today. This is just a social visit.

[*Revising again.*]

> No, I forgot my checkbook. But I'll be sure and bring it tomorrow.
> I just felt like saying hello.

[*Revising again.*]

> Oh, hell, I forgot it. I'll have to come back tomorrow.

[*He slips off his jacket, trying a casual pose.*]

Did you get enough to eat? Another margarita? . . . In that case, why don't I just take you home?

[*Revising.*]

You know, instead of going to get your car, why don't I just drive you straight home? A lot of bored cops on the road these days, waiting to pull someone over . . . I don't know. Let's do a little drunk test. Hold out your arms like this. Now, close your eyes. Now see if you can touch your nose . . . That does it. I'm driving you home.

[*Blackout.*]

SCENE EIGHT

[*Outside the house. Night.* CHARLIE *walks up to the sliding glass door with* CRYSTAL, *holding her elbow as if he's helping an old lady across the street.*]

CRYSTAL: Okay, I'm good now. Thanks.

CHARLIE: It's so dark out here.

CRYSTAL: That stupid bulb must have burned out.

CHARLIE: Nice house.

CRYSTAL: Thanks. I really like it here.

[*Pause. She holds out her hand for a handshake.*]

Well . . . thanks again for dinner. It's a pleasure working with you.

[*He laughs at this, and she joins in, lightly.*]

CHARLIE: Would you mind if I just came in and used your restroom?

CRYSTAL: . . . Oh. Sure.

CHARLIE: I'll be careful not to wake up your daughter.

CRYSTAL: Oh, she's not here . . . she's at a sleepover.

[*She starts automatically to reach for her ID card, but stops herself. At a loss, she feigns digging through her purse for an imaginary key.*]

Oh shit. I don't have my house key.

CHARLIE: That's a setback.

CRYSTAL: I must have left it in my car.

CHARLIE: Do you need me to break in?

CRYSTAL: No, I . . . , you know what? My roommate's probably here, he can let me in.

[*She starts knocking.*]

Gary! . . . Gary!

CHARLIE [*to himself*]: Roommate.

[GARY *comes down from upstairs looking worse than ever, disheveled and confused. He's holding the two-by-four.*]

CRYSTAL: Gary, it's me! Open the door!

[GARY *comes through the kitchen, stares at* CHARLIE, *and after an eternity, opens the door.* CHARLIE *offers* GARY *his hand.*]

CHARLIE: Sorry to wake you. Crystal forgot her key.

CRYSTAL: Gary, this is Charlie. He's a client from work.

[GARY *doesn't take* CHARLIE's *hand.*]

CHARLIE: So. Bathroom?

CRYSTAL: Straight ahead on your left.

[CHARLIE *exits.*]

Gary, I need you to be my helper again, okay? You're my room-mate, and you're a nice guy, not hostile; and—you know what? Just go back to bed. Go.

GARY: What's he doing here?

CRYSTAL: He gave me a ride. It's complicated. It's really good that he knows you're here, but now I need you to clear out, let me handle him.

GARY: Which of his parts do you plan to "handle"?

CRYSTAL: That's disgusting, please, just go—

GARY: I'll be listening.

CRYSTAL: Gary—

[*He goes upstairs and* CRYSTAL *composes herself as* CHARLIE *returns.* CHARLIE *takes the scenic route, peering into the living room and looking around.*]

I just moved in.

CHARLIE: That guy a friend of yours?

CRYSTAL: You know . . . he's more of a family friend. He's new in town. So I agreed to let him stay with us for a little while.

CHARLIE: He's a little strange.

CRYSTAL: Oh, he's only like that when you wake him up.

CHARLIE: I don't know if you really want him around your daughter, you know what I mean?

CRYSTAL [*softly*]: I know.

[*Pause.*]

CHARLIE: You mind if I sit down for a minute? I have a long ride home.

CRYSTAL: I'm sorry you went out of your way.

CHARLIE: No trouble. My back just locks up if I drive too much.

CRYSTAL: That's why you need that adjustable lumbar seat.

CHARLIE: I don't know. I might have blown my car budget tonight on all those margaritas.

[*Pause.*]

CRYSTAL: Can I get you a glass of water or anything?

CHARLIE: Sure.

CRYSTAL: I hope you don't have an early day tomorrow.

CHARLIE: No, just prep work for that keynote address I have on Monday.

CRYSTAL: Who is it for again?

CHARLIE: United Federation of Soybean Suppliers. It's a tri-state organization.

CRYSTAL: Wow.

CHARLIE: It's their quarterly meeting, and the theme is "Keeping Optimistic in Hard Times."

CRYSTAL: And you're the keynote speaker. That's amazing.

CHARLIE: It's a nice gig. I'm hoping they'll have me back sometime, because I also do a speech on relating sports trivia to your life.

CRYSTAL: What's your speech about? Is it like the Holiday Inn one?

CHARLIE: Kind of. It's called "Getting the Wealth of Your Dreams."

CRYSTAL: Can you do some of it for me?

CHARLIE: Sure, if you want to pay my speaker's fee—

CRYSTAL [*laughing*]: Oh, great—

CHARLIE: I'm serious. I do private sessions. See, the secret laws that allow you to create prosperity are simple to use. Anyone can do it; you just have to be ready to receive the transmission. But one of the laws is the "Law of Compensation." So in other words, I can't just give it away. You have to commit—emotionally, mentally, spiritually, and financially—or the laws won't work. You should think about doing some sessions with me, though. I could triple your commissions, overnight.

CRYSTAL: I'll think about it.

CHARLIE: I have powerful intuition about people, and I keep having this feeling like I was meant to meet you . . . like there's something I have to teach you . . . or maybe something you have to teach me.

CRYSTAL: Well, I don't have much of a budget for extras right now.

CHARLIE: Maybe we should work out a trade. Say, a dozen sessions for a new car?

CRYSTAL: If it was my car, instead of the dealer's, I'd be all over that.

CHARLIE: All over it, huh?

[*Pause.*]

CRYSTAL: More water?

CHARLIE: Sure. Unless you have something stronger. Your buddy upstairs looks like he might know where to score some weed.

CRYSTAL: You have a long ride home, so that's probably a bad idea.

CHARLIE: I actually drive better with a little something on board, you know what I mean?

CRYSTAL: Well, driving your new Sky Red Line is gonna be the best high you've ever had.

CHARLIE: This is starting to seem like kind of a hard sell, you know? I'm sick of hearing about the goddamned car.

CRYSTAL: Okay.

CHARLIE: Let me ask you this: If I had come in today and said, "Look, I've decided to go with a Honda instead," would you have still gone out to dinner with me?

[*Pause.*]

CRYSTAL: But it's so important right now to buy American.

CHARLIE: Is that your answer?

CRYSTAL: What's the question?

CHARLIE: I get it.

[*Pause.*]

The thing about the Honda dealership is, they're willing to negotiate.

CRYSTAL: What our customers have found is that the places that say they negotiate are really just jacking up the price to begin with, so that's the great thing about Saturn: total price transparency. We put it all right there on a sheet of paper.

CHARLIE: So in other words, you're not willing to negotiate.

CRYSTAL: . . . I might be able to throw in some free Saturn merchandise.

CHARLIE: Like what? A travel mug?

CRYSTAL: But if buying American is something that doesn't matter to you then I don't know what else I can say. If you want to buy something that came from a factory in Oki-saka–whatever, then go right ahead. But when you buy a Saturn you're buying American ingenuity and American jobs; from the person who hands you the keys all the way back to the guys on the line in Spring Hill, Tennessee; it's like a family. And when you buy a Saturn, you can feel yourself becoming a part of that family; we even do a little sort of "thing" when you buy a car, everyone on the floor stands around and does this . . .

CHARLIE: What?

CRYSTAL: Well, it's supposed to be a surprise.

CHARLIE: Tell me.

CRYSTAL: We just sing a little song.

CHARLIE: How does it go?

CRYSTAL: You need a lot of people to do it, and I'm a bad singer.

CHARLIE: Do you want me to buy this car?

CRYSTAL: . . . Yes.

CHARLIE: Then sing me a song.

[Hesitantly, she stands in front of him and sings the following, to the tune of "La Cucaracha." There's some humiliating choreography involving hand-clapping.]

CRYSTAL:

You bought a Saturn, you bought a Saturn,
Put our service to the test.
You bought a Saturn, you bought a Saturn,
Saturn owners are the best!
Go-o-o-o-o, Saturn!
Yay!

[*Pause.*]

CHARLIE: Not bad. Can you do that last part again?

CRYSTAL: Charlie, I don't think you're really undecided. I think you know exactly what you want to do. I've told you about the features of this car until I'm blue in the face—

CHARLIE: Stop right there. You see, I'm not really interested in the features. I'm interested in the benefits.

CRYSTAL: So you want to know how this car is going to change your life.

CHARLIE: Exactly.

CRYSTAL: Oh, Charlie. You've hit on the exact reason why I love selling cars. Because other than a house, I think a car is the single most life-enhancing purchase a person can make. Your car is like a second skin. You're in it every day. You live in it, you escape in it, you can even sleep in it . . . I've done that. If you have a family, it can change your relationship with your kids. If you're a single guy, it can be the thing that gets you laid. It's the face you show the world. It's you.

CHARLIE: Can you be more specific? How exactly is this car going to get me laid?

CRYSTAL: It's a really hot car. Women are going to love it.

CHARLIE: Like you, for example.

CRYSTAL: Obviously I think it's a great car.

CHARLIE: So if I buy this car, you'll be all over me like a cheap suit.

CRYSTAL: . . . I'm not really in the market these days for any kind of . . . romantic entanglements . . .

CHARLIE: Why? Because of that guy upstairs?

CRYSTAL: Oh, God no.

CHARLIE: So what's the problem? I took you out for a nice dinner and drove you home, but no, that's not enough for you. You want me to buy a car first.

CRYSTAL: It's not like that, I was just trying to help you make your decision—

CHARLIE: Just as a charity thing, out of the goodness of your heart. Because it's not like this sale is going to make your month or anything, oh no . . . I mean, that dealership is just *teeming* with customers . . .

CRYSTAL: Of course I want to make the sale, but I like you, Charlie, I'm just not—

CHARLIE: How much do you like me? Because I like you about thirty-two thousand, five hundred and ninety-four dollars plus tax. Do you want me to sign?

CRYSTAL: Yes I do.

CHARLIE: So where do we go? My place is no good. [*Indicating the living room*] In there?

[*She doesn't move.* GARY *comes in with his two-by-four.*]

GARY [*to* CHARLIE]: Get out.

CHARLIE: Easy there.

GARY: Get out before I hurt you.

CRYSTAL: Gary, don't be stupid; put that thing down—

CHARLIE [*to* CRYSTAL]: Let's go.

CRYSTAL: Gary, I wasn't—it wasn't what you think—

GARY [*to* CRYSTAL]: I heard what you said.

CRYSTAL: What am I supposed to do?

CHARLIE: I'm out of here. Are you coming?

[*She looks bewildered.*]

Last call.

GARY: Get the fuck out of here!

[GARY *lifts up the two-by-four, but* CRYSTAL *grabs his arm. She holds him for a moment in a sort of restraining embrace, looking into his face, keeping his arms at his sides.*]

CRYSTAL: Shhh. It's all going to be okay. I promise.

[*She lets go of him, grabs her purse, and leaves with* CHARLIE. *The sliding glass door closes.* GARY *flings the two-by-four after them. The glass cracks into a suspended bull's-eye. He starts opening the cabinets and flinging the contents around the room, creating as much destruction as he can. Blackout.*]

SCENE NINE

[*The dealership. The next morning.* SHANNON *is on the sales floor.* CRYS-TAL *enters, looking haggard.*]

SHANNON: Long night?

CRYSTAL: Kind of, why?

SHANNON: I just wondered, since you're wearing the exact same outfit you had on yesterday.

[CRYSTAL *looks at her with unveiled hostility.*]

CRYSTAL: Has anyone come by to drop off a check?

SHANNON: Today? No. But someone's here to see you.

CRYSTAL: Thank God.

[SHANNON *points out a middle-aged woman who's been standing some distance away, watching them and listening.*]

SHANNON: She was asking about you.

[CRYSTAL *approaches the woman with her hand out.*]

CRYSTAL: Hi, I'm Crystal. Is there a specific model you'd like to hear more about?

PATRICIA: Are you a friend of Charlie's?

[*Pause.*]

CRYSTAL: Did he send you here?

PATRICIA: No.

CRYSTAL: Are you—

PATRICIA: I'm his wife.

CRYSTAL: . . . Shannon, if you have a minute—

SHANNON [*standing very close*]: I do.

CRYSTAL: Great. Could you get me the keys for the Red Line XR?

SHANNON: Okay.

[SHANNON *exits.*]

CRYSTAL: What's your name?

PATRICIA: . . . Patricia.

CRYSTAL: Patricia. It's so nice to meet you. I know Charlie's been shopping for himself, but I think it's a great idea if you take the car for a test drive too—

PATRICIA: I'm not here about a car. I checked his GPS. I know he's been spending all this time here but when I ask him about his day he just tells me he's been at the library or the Y. He likes to have his secrets. I go easy on him. He got laid off eighteen months ago, and that's so hard on a man's ego. Now he wants to go around giving these "speeches," but honestly, no one will even give him the time of day; companies don't have money for that kind of silliness right now. We're okay, thank God; my investment advisor is a genius; but I know it hurts when he has to ask me for money just so he can pick up the dry cleaning. Let's not tell him I came here. I just . . . got nervous, I guess.

CRYSTAL: Sure.

PATRICIA: He didn't come home until two o'clock last night. He said he had a few drinks with an old friend and then his friend's car got towed . . . but I just had this feeling that his friend was not a man. I think he tells little lies sometimes, just so I won't get jealous. And I couldn't help hearing that you're wearing the same clothes you had on yesterday, so I think maybe you're the friend he was helping, is that right?

[SHANNON *returns with the keys.*]

SHANNON: Here you go.

CRYSTAL: Thank you.

PATRICIA: I had my car towed once, so I know what a pain it is, you have to get someone to drive you all the way across town . . . But he's that kind of guy. He makes friends wherever he goes. And I think for a man his age to spend time talking with pretty young women, maybe even flirting a little bit . . . if it makes him feel better about himself, there's nothing wrong with it.

CRYSTAL: Of course not.

PATRICIA: But now . . .

[SHANNON *is still there, listening.*]

I'm sorry, could you give us a minute please?

SHANNON: . . . Sure.

[SHANNON *exits.*]

PATRICIA: You might think this is really out of line, but I looked up his GPS addresses from last night and one of them is a motel. So I'm thinking it all makes sense, because maybe you couldn't get home for some reason because of the car situation, and he's a gentleman, he wouldn't go home until he was sure that you at least had a safe place to spend the night. The only thing that doesn't make sense is why he started coming here in the first place.

CRYSTAL: He's been looking at a Sky Red Line—

PATRICIA: That man. He's certainly not in the market for a new car; if anything, *I'm* the one who needs an upgrade; but my birthday is coming up next month, so for all I know, maybe he was planning some kind of surprise.

CRYSTAL: Well, it would be a shame if you—

PATRICIA: No, no, it doesn't matter, because we can't be buying that car. Whatever he had going on, I'm putting a stop to it right now.

CRYSTAL: You're making a big mistake.

PATRICIA: I don't think I am. I'm glad we had this talk. I feel so much better now. You see, the thing about Charlie is: he may be going through a rough patch right now, but at the end of the day, we've been through twenty-six years together, and I don't need him to buy me a car to show me how much he loves me.

[PATRICIA *starts to go.* CRYSTAL *watches as she heads for the door.*]

CRYSTAL: Patricia, I'm sorry, I can't let you walk out that door. It wouldn't be fair to you.

PATRICIA: No. We're done here.

CRYSTAL: I think you should know the truth.

PATRICIA: No, thank you—

CRYSTAL: I love him. With all my heart. And he loves me. We've been planning to run away together.

PATRICIA: No—

CRYSTAL: We've been planning it for months now.

PATRICIA: . . . No . . . that's not true—

CRYSTAL: I'm so sorry . . . I didn't know he was married, at least—not at first. We met at one of his speeches. We both tried to resist it, but he said he—he had this feeling like he was supposed to meet me. Like there was something we were supposed to teach each other. You know how he is . . . And he said—he said he couldn't bring himself to tell you. He was just going to leave a note.

[PATRICIA *is overcome.*]

But I have to tell you, Patricia, that until today, I would have thought that nothing in the world could keep us apart. It's just . . . so powerful. Only now that you're here, I can see how much you love him. And it makes me angry that he would do this to you.

PATRICIA: . . . It's not his fault; he's not himself right now—

CRYSTAL: No, you're right, it's not his fault. It's *my* fault. Because men—we know how they are, right? They're like children. And it's up to us to keep them on track, isn't it?

PATRICIA: I'm afraid so.

CRYSTAL: So what are we going to do?

[*Pause.*]

Patricia, this might sound crazy, but there's only one thing I can do. I see that now . . . I need to leave town. Just disappear and never see him again. Because if I stay, eventually we'll run into each other and the whole thing will start all over again.

PATRICIA: Where would you go?

CRYSTAL: Well, you see, that's the problem. I don't know. You see . . . I'm sorry—I'm just thinking out loud here . . . We've been planning to leave town *together* . . . So I sold my house at a huge loss, and I've given my notice here at work; I don't have any savings at all; but he said not to worry, he'd take care of everything.

PATRICIA: How did he think he was going to do that?

CRYSTAL: I don't know, but the point is: because of him, I have *nothing.*

[*Pause.*]

PATRICIA: Do you need me to buy you a bus ticket or . . .

CRYSTAL: Patricia, how would you manage if you took a bus to someplace where you didn't know anyone, and then got out and stood there with no money? No, it's not going to work. I'll just have to stay here and try my best to break it off with him. Promise me you won't worry, Patricia, because I hate to think of you sitting at home and worrying every time he's fifteen minutes late, worrying that he's with me. I would hate to think that I'm haunting you like that, maybe for years, maybe even for the rest of your life.

PATRICIA: How much do you need?

CRYSTAL: Well, let's see . . . first month's rent, food . . . and the job market is so terrible; I'm sure I'll be out of work for a long time . . .

PATRICIA: Five thousand?

CRYSTAL: That would be gone in a heartbeat. Plus there's child care; I have a daughter.

PATRICIA: Just say a number.

CRYSTAL: I don't see how I can do it for less than ten.

[PATRICIA *shakes her head.*]

You see? It's impossible. Excuse me. I'd better go beg for my job back.

PATRICIA: Assuming I could get it—and I have no idea if that's true—how soon would you be gone?

CRYSTAL: A few weeks.

[PATRICIA *makes a move to leave.*]

But if I had the money, let's say . . . tomorrow, I could do it a lot faster.

PATRICIA: I have to think.

CRYSTAL: Don't think too much about it, Patricia, or you'll start to hate me. I can tell you're a smart woman. If you really listen to yourself, I know you'll make the right choice.

[PATRICIA *exits.*]

SCENE TEN

[*Evening of the same day.* CRYSTAL *comes home. She sees the bull's-eye of broken glass in the sliding glass door. She pushes the door open. The kitchen is trashed. The word* WHORE *has been written in huge letters on the cabinets, daubed in some dark substance. She comes closer, trying to figure out what the substance is, and then quickly recoils. She's shaking. She finds paper towels and spray cleaner and starts cleaning off the cabinets.* GARY *comes in and watches her.*]

CRYSTAL: Why did you do this?

GARY: I don't know. I thought about a few other words but they had too many letters.

[*She keeps cleaning. He watches.*]

CRYSTAL: I thought I could trust you.

GARY: Yeah . . . Welcome home. Tough day at work?

[*She flings everything she can reach at him—the spray bottle and paper towels—missing him by a mile. For a moment, no one moves. She goes and picks up the things again and goes on cleaning.*]

You're lucky. I could have done so much more.

CRYSTAL: I've never been anything but kind to you.

GARY [*mimicking* CHARLIE *and* CRYSTAL]: "I don't know if he's the kind of guy you want around your daughter." "I know!"

CRYSTAL: I was just saying what he wanted to hear.

GARY: He was never gonna buy that car.

CRYSTAL: I didn't know that.

GARY: You're a terrible prostitute. Here's a tip: get the money up front next time.

CRYSTAL: Look: we've all done things we're not proud of. You need to get over it, or get out of this house.

GARY: No. You get out.

[*Pause.*]

CRYSTAL: Gary, let's both take a minute and count to ten. I don't want this to ruin our friendship.

GARY: Friendship. You crack me up.

CRYSTAL: It's true. Nothing's changed; I made a mistake, that's all.

GARY: Helen of Troy, Tokyo Rose. Fucking women. It's always the same thing: if I had a kid with you, I'd never know if it was mine.

CRYSTAL: Gary, please, I can't think about the future; I just need to focus on right now. We just have three more days until that lady comes back. You were so great before; can you please just help me a little while longer, and then I'll do anything you want, I promise—

GARY: Why are you always calling me Gary? That's not my name.

CRYSTAL: It's not?

GARY: That's just what it says in my underwear.

CRYSTAL: What's your real name?

GARY: I don't know.

[*Pause.*]

CRYSTAL: I think you need to eat something. Can I fix you some dinner?

[*She opens the refrigerator door, and a big mess of something flops and oozes out onto the floor.*]

GARY: Surprise.

[*She slams the door. She doesn't speak for a moment.*]

CRYSTAL: Why don't we go out and I'll buy you something to eat?

GARY: Negative.

CRYSTAL: Come on. I'll drive you. You won't even have to get out of the car.

GARY: You think I'm so stupid. You had me going for a while there. You're sick, you make me sick, you're a sickness. She needs a piece of the teacher, the greens are too much, but she can't eat, can't eat, she can't help it, she's gonna turn out just like you . . . Someone needs to help that little girl . . .

CRYSTAL: She needs your help, Gary, so why don't we go help her. We can go right now.

GARY: No way, no, no way, Mata Hari. Why do you want her so badly? What are you gonna do to her?

CRYSTAL: She needs me.

GARY: Nobody needs anyone, least of all you, fucking white-bread government whore.

CRYSTAL: That's not true.

GARY: We're done. Get out of my house.

[*She doesn't move.*]

Get out.

CRYSTAL: Please, Gary—

[*He suddenly runs at her, trying to push her out by force. She resists and pushes him off. He stares at her for a moment, shocked. He lunges at her again, trying to choke her. They grapple and struggle for a while, slipping on the detritus that still litters the floor. She manages to push him backward, and he falls, hitting his head against the edge of the counter. He lands on the ground. She grabs GARY's two-by-four off the counter and watches him. For a moment he doesn't move. Then he recovers and lunges at her again. Crystal hits him with the two-by-four until he falls, cringing. She goes over to him, lifts the two-by-four, and brings it down as hard as she can, bludgeoning him over and over until the end of the wood is tipped with blood. She staggers away and begins to clean up the kitchen.*]

CRYSTAL: Oh God.

[*She goes on cleaning. She looks back at GARY. She goes to him and looks at him closely.*]

CRYSTAL: Oh God oh God oh God—

[*She goes on cleaning. She stops, finds a blanket, and wraps Gary's dead body in it. Outside, the streetlight flicks on. She stares at it for a moment, then starts to drag the body, with great difficulty, out of the kitchen. Elsewhere lights also rise on* CHARLIE, *alone at his mirror.*]

CHARLIE: Let me tell you something: the hardest part of making your dreams come true is simply believing that you deserve it. The first time someone offered me these secrets, I was resistant. I couldn't accept what they had to offer, because deep down, I was afraid of my own personal potential. Now, that was stupid, wasn't it? We all have the power to manifest our own reality. Harness that power, and you'll find that the things you need appear in your life in ways you never could have imagined. And don't be afraid when this starts to happen. When a gift is offered to you, you should accept it.

[CRYSTAL *still goes on cleaning.*]

CHARLIE: And you tell yourself: this is the Universe taking care of me, giving me everything I deserve.

SCENE ELEVEN

[*Lights change. The Saturn dealership.* SHANNON *is alone, wearing a party hat and holding a drink and a balloon. She sings the Saturn song to herself, making up her own choreography, which is slightly more lascivious than* CRYSTAL*'s. While she sings,* CRYSTAL *enters.*]

SHANNON:
    You bought a Saturn, you bought a Saturn,
    Put our service to the test.
    You bought a Saturn, you bought a Saturn,
    Saturn owners are the best.
    Saturn . . .
    Working here is such a gas . . .

[*She sucks helium from the balloon.*]

    Till they fuck you in the ass.

[*She sees* CRYSTAL.]

    Crystal! Hey . . . Happy Last Day. Drinks are in the lounge.

[CRYSTAL *gives her a dazed stare and keeps going, back toward the offices.*]

Oh! Check your box. That lady dropped off an envelope for you.

[*Pause.*]

CRYSTAL: Thank you.

[CRYSTAL *exits.*]

SHANNON: Anytime.

SCENE TWELVE

[*The kitchen. Early evening, just before dusk.* TONI *and* CRYSTAL *sit at the kitchen table.* TONI *makes notes in a folder.* CRYSTAL *tries to sneak a glance at what she's writing, but* TONI *is casually positioned to prevent this. Finally she stops writing and closes the folder.*]

TONI: Everything looks good. And this is your lease?

[CRYSTAL *nods and slides some papers across the table to her.*]

"Joe Parker." Huh. I used to know a fellow by that name.

[*She shrugs and tucks the lease into the file. They look at each other for a moment.*]

CRYSTAL: So what's next?

TONI: We're done.

CRYSTAL: Done?

TONI: I'll tell my supervisor you've remediated all the problems we discussed. And I'll recommend reinstatement of custody.

CRYSTAL: So I can go get her?

TONI: The judge needs to sign off first, and then we'll schedule a time. It'll take about a day or two.

[*Pause.*]

Crystal? Are you all right? I know it's hard, dealing with all this. It probably seems like it's been going on forever.

[CRYSTAL *can't speak.* TONI *pats her on the hand.*]

Look at everything you've done. You've turned your whole life around.

CRYSTAL: I'd do anything for her.

TONI: I know you would.

[*Pause.*]

Well. I'd better get on the road. Three more stops on my way home. Goddamned budget cuts.

[*They get up and move to the sliding glass door.* TONI *sees the splintered bull's-eye in the glass.*]

CRYSTAL: Oh . . . I forgot to tell you . . . I'm getting this fixed. They're coming tomorrow.

TONI: Bird?

CRYSTAL: Pardon?

TONI: Did a bird fly into it?

CRYSTAL: Yes. It was so sad.

[TONI *steps outside.*]

TONI: Take care now.

[CRYSTAL *manages a polite half-smile but doesn't answer. She stands framed in the doorway, watching* TONI *leave. She waves as* TONI *drives away. It's darker out now. For a long moment,* CRYSTAL *seems frozen, almost catatonic, rooted in the doorway. The streetlight blinks on. She stares at it. She slides the door closed and locks it. Blackout.*]